The Battle of Griswoldville: An Infantry Battle on Sherman's March to the Sea

Robert C. Jones

Robert C. Jones
POB 1775
Kennesaw, Georgia 30156

jone442@bellsouth.net
rcjbooks.com

"The Battle of Griswoldville: An Infantry Battle on Sherman's March to the Sea", Copyright 2011 by Robert C. Jones. All rights reserved.

First Edition

ISBN: 1461164214
EAN-13: 978-1461164210

Table of Contents

Introduction..4
Background - The March to the Sea..5
    Sherman's strategy...7
Feint on Macon..11
The Antagonists at Griswoldville...15
    Major General Joseph Wheeler, CSA..15
    Brigadier General Judson Kilpatrick, USA...................................16
    Brigadier General Charles Robert Woods, USA.......................18
    Brigadier General Pleasant Jackson Philips, CSA 19
    Brigadier General Charles Walcutt, USA....................................19
    Colonel Robert Catterson, USA..21
    Major General Gustavus Woodson Smith, CSA.......................22
Battles for Griswoldville 24
    November 20, 1864...24
    November 21, 1864...25
    November 22, 1864 - morning..26
    Battle of Griswoldville...27
Assessment of the Battle of Griswoldville......................................34
Sherman's March to the Sea – End Game and Aftermath............37
    Results..40
Griswoldville Battlefield today..41
Appendix A – The Destruction of Griswoldville............................42
Appendix B - Descriptions of the Battle from the Official Record..............44
Sources..48
The Author on YouTube...49
About the Author...50

Introduction

Love him or hate him, the actions of William Tecumseh Sherman in Georgia in 1864 transformed the Civil War in the space of seven months. From a conflict which was still very much in doubt as to its victor in early 1864, by the time Sherman had captured Atlanta, marched to the Sea, and captured Savannah, the will to fight had largely left the South, and the outcome of the War had become a foregone conclusion.

This book tells the story of what is sometimes described as the only infantry battle on Sherman's March – the Battle of Griswoldville. It is the tale of an inexperienced Georgia Militia general ordering an attack across an open, boggy field against an entrenched brigade of Sherman's troops. It is the tale of the bravery of the young boys and old men on that charge, some who had been pressed into emergency service just before the battle. It is the tale of the horror of the Union troops when they examined the dead and wounded, and discovered that many were 15 or younger, and what today we would describe as "senior citizens". It is the tale of a small manufacturing city that was fought over for <u>three days</u>, changing hands several times.

I hope you enjoy this look at what is today an obscure but fierce battle fought during Sherman's March to the Sea.

- Robert Jones, Kennesaw Georgia, May 2011

Background - The March to the Sea

c. 1868 engraving showing "Sherman's march to the sea"[1]

> NOVEMBER 15-DECEMBER 21, 1864. - The Savannah (Georgia) Campaign.
> On the 12th of November my army stood detached and cut off from all communication with the rear. It was composed of four corps-the Fifteenth and Seventeenth, constituting the Right wing, under Major General O. O. Howard; the Fourteenth and Twentieth Corps, constituting the Left Wing, under Major General H. W. Slocum-of an aggregate strength of 60,000 infantry; one cavalry division, in aggregate strength 5,500 under Brigadier General Judson Kilpatrick, and the artillery, reduced to the minimum, one gun per 1,000 men. (Sherman to Grant)[2]

Even today, Sherman's March to the Sea can excite opprobrium on the part of people in the South, especially in Georgia. It was a new kind of warfare – warfare against civilian as well as military/industrial targets. Sherman might be viewed as the first proponent of "total war". Sherman's view was that the Civil War could not have started without the fervent support of the Southern

---

[1] Library of Congress http://www.loc.gov/pictures/item/2003679761
[2] *War of the Rebellion: Official Records of the Union and Confederate Armies*, U.S. Government Printing Office, 1891

civilian population, and now it was time for them to "pay the piper".

William Tecumseh Sherman[3]

Sherman's March was also something new in warfare where a large modern army *on purpose* destroyed its own supply lines, and decided to live off the land for several weeks. Sherman had experimented with the idea during the Atlanta Campaign when he veered away from the Western & Atlantic Railroad to avoid fighting at Allatoona Pass, thus resulting in the battles of Dallas, New Hope Church, Pickett's Mill, etc. But he eventually returned to the W&A, and set up a supply depot at Big Shanty to prepare for the great battle at Kennesaw Mountain. During the March to the Sea, there would be no supply line for Union troops until they linked up with Union ships in Savannah.

---

[3] Library of Congress http://www.loc.gov/pictures/item/94512493

Another interesting feature of the March was the fact that there was no significant organized resistance at any point along the 275 mile corridor in central Georgia until Sherman's 62,000 man army faced 10,000 Confederates under Hardee in Savannah. Arrayed against Sherman was Wheeler's cavalry force of 3,500, which could annoy Sherman's army, and even win a couple of small battles versus Sherman's cavalry under Judah Kilpatrick, but these battles had absolutely no impact on Sherman reaching his objective, which was Savannah. Also arrayed against Sherman was about 2,700 members of the Georgia Militia under General Gutavus Smith, some members of the Georgia Military Institute, and about a thousand members of the "Orphan's Brigade" – Confederates from Kentucky.

John Bell Hood's army was in Tennessee, and was being diligently pursued by half of Sherman's army under "Rock of Chickamauga" General George Thomas. Sherman had a clear path to Savannah. Sherman's March was not a series of battles, as Sherman's Atlanta Campaign was; rather, it was a three week search for food and supplies over a 275 mile route.

Sherman's strategy

After capturing Atlanta in September of 1864, why did Sherman decide that it was necessary to sweep through central Georgia to the coast? Among the reasons:

- Sherman wanted to directly involve the civilian population of Georgia in the war, feeling that civilians from Georgia were as responsible for the War as Confederate leaders and military officers
- As Sherman destroyed the Western and Atlantic in November of 1864, he wanted to destroy the railroads in central Georgia as well. This included the Georgia Railroad and the Georgia Central Railroad.
- Sherman figured that cutting a swathe of destruction though the heart of the Confederacy would have a devastating effect on Southern morale

- By taking Savannah, Sherman could link up with the Union navy and its supply ships

In the official record, Sherman discusses how his March divided the Confederate forces in Georgia:

> My first object was, of course, to place my army in the very heart of Georgia, interposing between Macon and Augusta, and obliging the enemy to divide his forces to defend not only those points, but Millen, Savannah, and Charleston. All my calculations were fully realized.
>
> ...it will suffice here to state that the important city of Savannah, with its valuable harbor and river, was the chief object of the campaign.[4]

During the March, Sherman sent feints towards both Macon and Augusta, which were obviously successful as the following newspaper article testifies:

> Our information from Georgia in regard to Sherman is meager. All that we know certainly is that he left Atlanta about one week ago with a force generally estimated at 30,000 men of all arms, and that **he was moving in the direction of Macon**...He moves slowly, and ere he reaches Macon he will find that the execution of a plan is quite a different thing from its projection.
>
> LATER. --We hear that Sherman has divided his army. **He has sent nearly all his mounted force in the direction of Augusta**; with his main body of troops, he himself marches on to Macon. (Richmond *Examiner*; emphasis added[5])

---

[4] *Official Record*
[5] *Ibid*

This c. 1906 photo shows the the only remains of the Augusta Powder Works – the chimney from the Sibley Mill. The chimney still stands today, and has been recently restored.[6]

It is the feint towards Macon which will figure most prominently in the Battle of Griswoldville.

---

[6] Library of Congress http://www.loc.gov/pictures/item/det1994013530/PP/

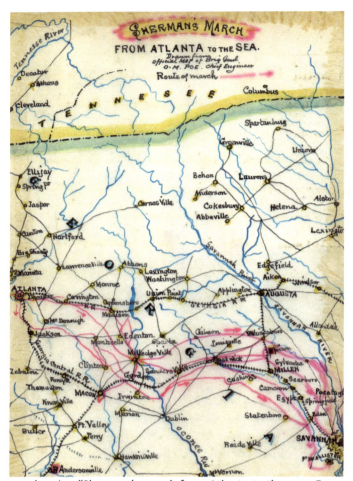

1864 map showing "Sherman's march from Atlanta to the sea. Drawn from official map of Brig. Genl. O. M. Poe, Chief Engineer." Griswoldville is located between Macon and Gordon on the map, in the lower left-hand corner.[7]

---

[7] Library of Congress http:hdl.loc.gov/loc.ndlpcoop/gvhs01.vhs00040

Feint on Macon

In the early days of Sherman's March, one of the objectives was to make the Southern troops think that his objective was Macon, not Savannah. His instrument for carrying out this strategy was Judson Kilpatrick's cavalry.

On November 15, Kilpatrick's cavalry headed south from Atlanta and drove Wheeler's cavalry from Jonesboro. Wheeler retreated to Lovejoy, and temporarily joined with the Georgia Militia troops stationed there (about 2,700 strong), under the command of General Gustavus Smith. Kilpatrick then overwhelmed the Confederate position at Lovejoy and Hampton, to which the retreating militia and Wheeler's cavalry had fled. The Confederate militia and cavalry retreated to Griffin.

On November 19, Joe Wheeler's cavalry arrived in Macon to protect the town from Kilpatrick's cavalry. Fighting occurred in and around Macon on November 20-21 1864.

> General Kilpatrick waited at Clinton until the arrival of the head of the infantry column, at 12 m., when he moved out toward Macon on the left Macon road. He met the enemy's cavalry about four miles from Macon, drove them in, and charged their works, defended by infantry and artillery. The head of his column got inside the works, but could not hold them. He succeeded in reaching the railroad and destroyed about one mile of the track. The road was struck in two or three places by the cavalry, besides the above, and a train of cars burned. (O. O. Howard, Major-General)[8]

---

[8] *Official Record*

Confederate artillery battery at Riverside Cemetery. The battery is (essentially) the "Pine Fort" section of the cemetery.

Many Confederate officials, military and civilian, were in Macon at the time of Kilpatrick's attack, including Generals Wheeler and Smith, Howell Cobb, Robert Toombs, Lieutenant General Richard Taylor and General William Joseph Hardee. After the War, General Gustavus Smith commented on the number of generals in Macon, perhaps slightly ironically:

> When my command reached Macon, the workshop troops, home guards, local reserve cavalry, and the artillery — except Anderson's battery— were ordered to report to General Cobb. In the meantime General Beauregard, Lieutenant-Generals Hardee and Richard Taylor, and other officers of prominence, reached Macon, but they brought no troops with them. General Hardee assumed the chief command. (Gustavus W. Smith[9])

---

[9] *Battles and Leaders of the Civil War Volume Four*, by Robert Underwood Johnson and Clarence Clough Buel (New York, Century Co., 1888)

Soldier's Square at Rose Hill Cemetery. Some Confederate soldiers killed at Griswoldville are buried in this cemetery.

By November 21. Hardee had figured out that the real target of Sherman's March was not Macon, and he cautiously starting dispersing troops that had been defending Macon to Augusta and Savannah.

> SAVANNAH, November 23, 1864.
> General S. COOPER:
> Adjutant and Inspector General:
> I left Macon Monday night for this place, via Fort Valley, Albany, and Thomasville, and reached here tonight. When I left Macon I could hear of no enemy west of the Ocmulgee. The enemy had not been at Forsyth, Griffin, or Barnesville. It was believed that Sherman was moving with his main force on Augusta. I could, however, gain no definite or reliable information respecting the movements of the enemy's infantry. Wheeler attacked the enemy's cavalry at Clinton Sunday's, but gained no advantage and got no information. The same day Colonel Crews drove the enemy from Griswold, but being re-enforced, Crews was in turn driven from the place. Monday Wheeler advanced on Griswold and drove Kilpatrick, who retreated on Milledgeville. Believing Macon would not be attacked, in which my principal officers concurred, I ordered General Smith's entire force, and a part of Cobb's, to move on Augusta via the Central railroad. This road was broken, but as far as heard from could be easily repaired.

Lieutenant - General Taylor was in Columbus Monday, and was expected at Macon Tuesday following, and would assume command. W. J. Hardee, Lieutenant – General.[10]

Lieutenant – General William J. Hardee, CSA[11]

---

[10] *Official Record*
[11] Library of Congress http://www.loc.gov/pictures/item/00652519/

The Antagonists at Griswoldville

Major General Joseph Wheeler, CSA

Major General Joseph Wheeler (1836-1906)[12]

Joseph Wheeler was, along with Nathan Bedford Forrest, the most significant Confederate cavalry officer in the West during the Civil War. Wheeler fought in a number of battles and raids throughout the War, including Shiloh, the Chickamauga Campaign, the Tullahoma Campaign, the Chattanooga Campaign, the Knoxville Campaign, Sherman's Atlanta Campaign and March to the Sea, and the Carolinas Campaign. He was a key player in the defeat of the Stoneman Raid into central Georgia in July of 1864.

---

[12] Library of Congress http://www.loc.gov/pictures/item/cwp2003000446/PP/

Later, Wheeler served as a major general of volunteers in the Spanish American War, and had Theodore Roosevelt's Rough Riders under his campaign.

Wheeler was the sole Confederate (as opposed to Militia) fighting force that challenged Sherman during the March to the Sea. Most of his battles with Sherman were with his opposing number, Judson Kilpatrick, but a couple of times he had Union infantry arrayed against him (Griswoldville, Waynesboro). He successfully helped defend Macon against a Cavalry Raid by Kilpatrick in the early days of the March 1864.

Brigadier General Judson Kilpatrick, USA

Brigadier General Judson Kilpatrick (1836-1881)[13]

---

[13] Library of Congress http://www.loc.gov/pictures/item/brh2003002881/PP/

Judson Kilpatrick was one of the most flamboyant of all Union cavalry officers during the Civil War. He was an expert at destroying railroad infrastructure, especially in central Georgia during Sherman's March to the Sea.

Judson first gained fame for being part of the Stoneman Raid during the Battle of Chancellorsville. While the Union suffered an ignominious loss at Chancellorsville, the Raid was a success. He later fought at Gettysburg.

In the Spring of 1864, he led an unsuccessful raid to free the Union prisoners held at Belle Isle and Libby prisons. Later, Kilpatrick was transferred to the Army of the Cumberland under William Tecumseh Sherman. He fought in the early part of Sherman's Atlanta Campaign, until he was wounded at the Battle of Resaca. After recovering, he once completely circled Atlanta during the siege of said city in August, 1864.

His greatest fame would come for his role in Sherman's March to the Sea, a campaign in which he had 5,500 men under his command. Kilpatrick's cavalry made a feint towards Macon in the early part of the March, making the Confederates think that Macon was Sherman's target. Later in the March, he made a similar feint towards Augusta. He fought in repeated battles with Confederate cavalry general Joseph Wheeler (Griswoldville, Macon, Waynesboto). On November 27, 1864 it appears that Kilpatrick was enjoying the attentions of a lady friend near Sylvan Grove, when he was roused half-clothed from bed, and had to flee from Wheeler's cavalry. Later in the fighting, Union infantry had to bail out Kilpatrick's cavalry as the latter was fleeing from Wheeler.

In 1865, Kilpatrick was appointed Minister to Chile by President Andrew Johnson.

Brigadier General Charles Robert Woods, USA

Brigadier General Charles Robert Woods (1827-1885)[14]

Charles Woods was involved in the Civil War from its earliest days – he was charged with leading 200 reinforcements to Fort Sumter in 1861. Because of heavy firing from Confederate shore batteries, he was unsuccessful and retreated.

Woods did most of his fighting in the West. He participated in the battles at Fort Donelson, Chickasaw Bayou, Vicksburg and Chattanooga. It was one of his brigades that held off the Confederate attack at Griswoldville during Sherman's March to the Sea.

---

[14] Library of Congress http://www.loc.gov/pictures/item/cwp2003004202/PP/

Woods was recognized by the U.S. Senate for his role in the Battle of Griswoldville:

> Brigadier-General Charles R. Woods, of the United States Volunteers, for long and continued services and for special gallantry at Griswoldville, Georgia, to date from November 22, 1864 (Senate Executive Journal – Monday, January 30, 1865)[15]

Brigadier General Pleasant Jackson Philips, CSA

Pleasant Jackson Philips (1819–1876) was a Georgia plantation owner and banker before the Civil War. He became a Brigadier General in the Georgia Militia in 1862. He served briefly in Virginia. In 1864, he participated in the Battle of Atlanta.

During the March to the Sea, he was given orders on November 22, 1864 to take a force of Georgia Militia to Griswoldville, and wait for further orders. After arriving at Gridwoldville, he launched an attack on a Federal brigade entrenched on a ridge line. His forces were soundly defeated.

After the disaster at Griswoldville, Philips retired from the military. He eventually returned to his banking career in Columbus, Georgia.

I have never seen a photo or drawing of General Philips. If you know of one, please contact me!

Brigadier General Charles Walcutt, USA

Walcutt's first major battle was at Shiloh, where he was wounded in the shoulder. He fought at Vicksburg, Jackson, and Chattanooga, where he assumed command of his brigade when the brigade commander, John Corse, was injured.

Walcutt fought in Sherman's Atlanta Campaign, and was promoted to Brigadier General during the Campaign.

---

[15] Library of Congress http://memory.loc.gov/cgi-bin/query/D?hlaw:1:./temp/~ammem_7dMg::

Brigadier General Charles Walcutt (1838-1898)[16]

Walcutt is probably most famous for his participation as a brigade commander at the Battle of Griswoldville on November 22, 1864. His brigade held the line against a superior force of Georgia Militia. Walcutt was injured again during this battle, and was out of action for weeks.

Walcutt was recognized by the U.S. Senate for his bravery at Griswoldville:

> Brigadier-General Charles C. Walcott, of the United States Volunteers, for special gallantry at the battle of Griswoldville, Georgia... (Senate Executive Journal - Tuesday, February 6, 1866)[17]

---

[16] Library of Congress http://www.loc.gov/pictures/item/cwp2003004150/PP/
[17] Library of Congress http://memory.loc.gov/cgi-bin/query/D?hlaw:2:./temp/~ammem_7dMg::

Colonel Robert Catterson, USA

Colonel Robert Catterson (1835-1914)[18]

Robert Catterson was a doctor who eventually rose to the rank of Brigadier General (he was a colonel during the Battle of Griswoldville). Earlier in the War, he served in the Maryland Campaign and at the Battle of Antietam, where he was wounded. He later participated in the battle for Vicksburg, the Tullahoma Campaign, Chattanooga and the Atlanta Campaign in 1864.

When Charles Walcutt was injured about an hour into the Battle of Griswoldville, Catterson took over command, and successfully repelled the Georgia Militia attack.

---

[18] Library of Congress http://www.loc.gov/pictures/item/cwp2009000008/PP/

After the War, he fought against the Klu Klux Klan in Arkansas, and became a US Marshall.

Major General Gustavus Woodson Smith, CSA

Major General Gustavus Woodson Smith[19]

Gustavus Smith has the most varied resume of our Griswoldville combatants. Smith was the head of the Army of Northern Virginia for one day, after Joseph Johnston was seriously injured, and before Robert E. Lee took command. He served in the battles at Fair Oaks and Seven Pines. In 1862, he was put in charge of the defenses of Richmond. In November of 1862, he served as the interim Confederate Secretary of War.

---

[19] Library of Congress http://www.loc.gov/pictures/item/2002705763/

Smith served as the superintendent of the Etowah Iron Works in 1863-1864

In 1863 and 1864, he served as the superintendent of the Etowah Iron Works in Georgia. In June of 1864, he was appointed a major general in the Georgia State Militia, , and was the head of the state militia during the time of Sherman's March. Under orders from Hardee, Smith began sending Georgia Militia units from Macon towards Augusta on November 21 and November 22, 1864, when it became apparent that Macon was not the target of Sherman's March. He sent Pleasant Philips towards Griswoldville, with orders to wait for further instructions, and not to engage the enemy. The Battle of Griswoldville would be the result.

Battles for Griswoldville

Griswoldville, or Griswold Station as it was sometimes called, was a small manufacturing town founded by Samuel Griswold. Griswold choose the site because it was located on the Central Railroad. After the fall of Atlanta, the new headquarters of the Western & Atlantic Railroad was established in Griswoldville, GA in late-September 1864.

In 1862, Griswold began producing pistols for the Confederacy, using a converted cotton gin as his factory. In time, the pistol factory would produce about 3,500[20] pistols for the Confederate cause. The most common pistol manufactured was a six shot .36 caliber weapon. This pistol factory, as well as the railroad itself, became prime targets for Sherman's troops during the early days of the March to the Sea.

The fight for Griswoldville would last three days, and started with two days of cavalry clashes on November 20/21.

November 20, 1864

After Kilpatrick's attack (feint) on Macon was repulsed, he pulled back towards Griswoldville (about 10 miles east of Macon), destroying the railroad along the way. At 10:00a on November 20, Kilpatrick ordered Captain Ladd of the Ninth Michigan Volunteer Cavalry to take a 100 men to destroy public and railroad infrastructure in Griswoldville. The story of Ladd's Raid is probably worth at least a TV movie, but I suspect that *Raid on Griswoldville* wouldn't be as catchy a name as *The Guns of Navarone* or *Raid on Entebbe*.

> In the forenoon of this day, by order of General Kilpatrick, I sent 100 picked men of the Ninth Michigan Volunteer Cavalry, under Captain Ladd, of that regiment, to Griswoldville, with orders to burn public buildings and destroyed the railroad. Starting from Clinton he found the enemy picketing the roads. Avoiding them to kept on trough the woods, reached Griswoldville, and charged

---
[20] Some sources say 3,700

into the town, driving the enemy out, and under their fire captured and burned a locomotive and train of cars; burned the public buildings, and destroyed the railroad. After this work was accomplished he captured one of the enemy, and compelled him to lead his little party out of the town on a route to avoid the enemy, who had all the roads in their possession. The gallant conduct of Captain Ladd and his brave troopers is a fine example of what a few men can accomplish when daringly and persistently led. Smith D. Atkins, Colonel Ninety-second Illinois Infantry, Mounted, Commanding Brigade. Captain L. G. ESTES, Assistant Adjutant-General.[21]

Kilpatrick later described in more detail what Ladd's men had destroyed in Griswoldville:

A detachment of Ninth Michigan Cavalry, Captain Ladd commanding, had already struck the railroad at Griswold Station, capturing a train of thirteen cars, loaded with engine driving wheels and springs for same. The station was destroyed; pistol, soap and candle factories burned. (J. Kilpatrick, Brigadier-General, Commanding Cavalry). [22]

Ladd lost three men captured and 1 wounded.

After Ladd's men left Griswoldville, Wheeler's cavalry briefly retook the city. Kilpatrick's cavalry then drove Wheeler's men out, leaving Griswoldville in possession of the Yankees the evening of November 20.

November 21, 1864

On November 21, Kilpatrick's men continued destroying the railroad line in and near Griswoldville. Kilpatrick (like Wheeler before him) used the mansion of Samuel Griswold as his headquarters.

Wheeler launched a cavalry assault on Griswoldville, and retook the town, taking a few prisoners in the process. Wheeler's men

---

[21] *Official Record*
[22] *Ibid*

camped in Griswoldville that night. Three Union cavalry regiments camped just east of Grisdwoldville, near Little Sandy Creek.

Meanwhile, back in Macon, Hardee had figured out that Macon was not Sherman's primary target, and guessed that Sherman's target was actually the powder mills in Augusta. Hardee ordered Brigadier General Reuben W. Carswell's First Brigade of Georgia Militia to march towards Gordon, where he hoped that they would be able to board trains for Augusta. Gordon had already been taken by Sherman's forces at that time, but Hardee didn't know it.

November 22, 1864 - morning

Wheeler attacked the Union cavalry east of Griswoldville at 7am and "drove the enemy for some distance, capturing sixty prisoners, besides killing and wounding a large number" (Joseph Wheeler)[23]. Wheeler was repelled by a Union cavalry brigade and an infantry brigade under Brigadier General Charles Walcutt, part of the division of Charles Woods. Wheeler was gone from Griswoldville by 10am.

The reason that Walcutt's brigade was in Griswoldville is because the morning of November 22, the brigades of Brigadier General Charles Wood were ordered to make a "demonstration" toward Griswoldville.

> Your orders for the 22nd of November were to make a demonstration against Griswoldville, while our trains [supplies] were to be pushed on toward Gordon with all the dispatch the terrible condition of the rutted roads permitted. I consequently ordered one brigade (General Walcutt's) of General Wood's division to move early on the south side of the railroad in the direction of Griswoldville. When I joined General Walcutt to accompany the expedition, [with] General Kilpatrick's in his front, and a portion of it, which had tried to drive back the rebel advance line, had just come back without having succeeded. General Walcutt was ordered at once to relieve the cavalry, and the advance was sounded. A strong line of skirmishers, supported by two regiments and some cavalry, which General Kilpatrick had

---

[23] *Official Record*

kindly furnished, soon struck the rebels, who were in line behind a creek, or rather swamp, in an open pine land, and caused them, with that peculiar spirit of our troops, to look for their horses and run. General Walcutt kept pushing forward, and his men pursued in double-quick with cheers and laughter the fleeing horsemen, waded the creek, marched through the belt of timber beyond until they reached an open prairie like field, which was in possession of large rebel cavalry forces. General Walcutt halted here just long enough to correct his line, caution his skirmishers and supports to be prepared for a cavalry dash, and then they emerged into the open field and made for the rebels, who, throwing away the best chance that can be desired by an intrepid cavalry, fled in confusion General Walcutt followed rapidly, capturing many horses, equipments, &c. When beyond Griswoldville the rebels, who were commanded by General Wheeler in person, took different roads; and as I had some knowledge of Wheeler's way of maneuvering- which is not formidable in the dash of arms, but sometimes successful by great activity and circumspection - I ordered General Woods to have General Walcutt's command rallied and take a defensive position near the open field mentioned above. (P. Jos. Osterhaus, Major-General, U. S. Volunteers.)

The presence of Walcutt's brigade at Griswoldville set the stage for the Battle of Griswoldville.

Battle of Griswoldville

I have the honor to report that the affair of yesterday at Duncan's farm, near Griswold, was of greater magnitude than was at first supposed. (Chas. R. Woods, Brigadier-General of Volunteers[24])

The battle of Griswoldville will be remembered as an unfortunate accident whose occurrence might have been avoided by the exercise of proper caution and circumspection. It in no wise crippled the movements of the enemy, and entailed upon the Confederates a loss which, under the circumstances, could be illy sustained. (Colonel Charles Colcock Jones, General Hardee's Chief of Artillery)[25]

---

[24] *Official Record*
[25] *The Siege of Savannah*, by Charles Colcock Jones (Joel Munsell, 1874)

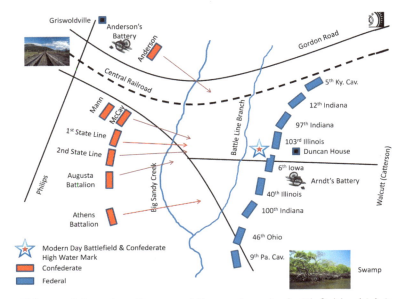

This map is based on the map at the modern-day battlefield, which is, unfortunately, worn to the point of non-readability. (Map by Robert C. Jones)

Brigadier General Charles Woods ordered Walcutt's brigade to entrench at Duncan's Farm (actually purchased by Samuel Griswold 15 years before) about 1.5 miles east of Griswoldville, to protect Union Supply lines from further assaults by Wheeler's Cavalry. Duncan's farm site was chosen as a defensive position as it commanded the road to Irwington. It also was on a rise, overlooking an open field that had a swampy creek (Little Sandy Creek) and a branch of the creek running through it. The position was protected by swamp on the left flank, as well as a railroad cut on the right flank.

The Union forces had about 1,500 men (a single brigade) dug into the heights on the Duncan Farm. Walcutt's superior, Charles Woods, describes the Union forces:

> Fortieth Illinois Infantry, Lieutenant Colonel H. W. Hall commanding, 206 enlisted men

Forty-sixth Ohio Infantry, Lieutenant Colonel I. N. Alexander commanding, 218 enlisted men
One hundred and third Illinois Infantry, Major A. Willison commanding, 219 enlisted men
Sixth Iowa Infantry, Major W. H. Clune commanding, 177 enlisted men
Ninety-seventh Indiana Infantry, Colonel R. F. Cattarson commanding, 366 enlisted men
One hundredth Indiana Infantry, Major R. M. Johnson commanding, 327 enlisted me
Total present for duty, 1,513
One section [two cannons] of Battery B. First Michigan, Captain Arndt commanding.[26]

Back in Macon, General Hardee, once he had figured out that Macon wasn't the real target of Sherman's March, ordered that the Georgia Militia troops defending Macon be sent to Augusta and Savannah. Major General Gustavus Woodson Smith, in charge of all Georgia Militia, then ordered Brigadier General Pleasant Jackson Philips to march with three brigades towards Griswoldville and wait for further instructions. Philips left Macon around 8:00a.

Philips was a Columbus banker that had little combat experience. However, he was the highest ranking Georgia Militia officer in Macon at the time, other than Smith himself. Smith had stayed behind in Macon, ostensibly to arrange for movement of supplies out of Macon towards Augusta and Savannah.

Philips reached the outskirts of Griswoldville from the west at around 1:00p. He linked up with 400 men of Major F.W.C. Cook's Reserve battalions. Cook's soldiers were primarily composed of workers from an armory in Athens, and a powder works in Augusta. Cook had earlier been ordered to Augusta by Hardee.

General Smith received a report from Cook stating that large portions of Sherman's army were still in the Griswoldville area. He probably realized with horror that he had sent the state militia into direct contact with Sherman's far superior force. He sent a courier

---

[26] *Official Record*

to Griswoldville to order Cook and Philips to return to Macon. The courier arrived just as the battle was starting.

Charge on the heights. This drawing was made at Kelly Ford, Virginia, but I thought it captured many of the elements of the Battle of Griswoldville – charging heights through a swamp, etc.[27]

In the 2:30-3:00p time frame, Philips ordered an attack across an open field at Duncan's farm against a (lightly) entrenched Federal position on the heights about 400 yards away. Philips's forces outnumbered the Federals by about 2:1[28], and he had 4 guns to only 2 for the Union. He probably figured that the advantage was on his side.

The Militia infantry spread out across the open field in this order:

- The aforementioned Cook attacked Walcutt's left
- Lieutenant Colonel Beverly D. Evans' State Line regiments and Brigadier General Henry Kent McCay's 4th Militia Brigade attacked the Union center. Many of the State Line soldiers had initially served as guards on the Western & Atlantic Railroad[29]. Some had seen action during the Atlanta Campaign.
- Brigadier General Charles D. Anderson's Third Militia attacked Walcutt's right

---

[27] Library of Congress http://www.loc.gov/pictures/item/2004661205/
[28] Philips had over 3,000 troops at the time of the attack to about 1,500 for the Federals
[29] William Fuller, the W&A conductor who had chased the *General* for 87 miles during the Great Locomotive Chase, was a Captain in the Independent State Guards. He was not present at Griswoldville.

- The Second Militia Brigade under Colonel James Mann was held in reserve

12-pounder Napoleon[30]

The Militia forces had four 12-pounder Napoleons, led by Captain Ruel W. Anderson of the 14th Georgia Light Artillery. As the battle opened, The Militia artillery proved to be deadly accurate, immediately destroying a Federal caisson, and taking the 2 Union guns out of action.

---

[30] Library of Congress http://www.loc.gov/pictures/item/2004661820/

Exploding caisson[31]

After the initial artillery barrage, the Militia began the famed Rebel yell, and moved forward towards a swampy creek that ran through the Duncan Farm. As the Militia got closer to the Union lines, Walcutt order his infantry to open fire.

Not surprisingly, the Militia attack bogged down in the swampy area around the creek. The poorly trained Militia were forced to fire uphill, and were generally ineffective. A Union regiment equipped with the seven-shot Spencer repeating rifles laid down a deadly fire against the approaching Confederates.

Cook's men and men of the State Line briefly threatened the Union left, but were pushed back when some of McCay's men mistakenly started firing on them.[32]

The attacking Southerners found some cover in a small ravine at the foot of the heights. There was really nowhere else for them to go. They couldn't flank the Federals because of the swamps and the railroad cut, and they couldn't retreat because they would have been slaughtered.

---
[31] Library of Congress http://www.loc.gov/pictures/item/2004660966/
[32] *Griswoldville*, by William Harris Bragg, p. 134

Walcutt was injured by a shell fragment in his right calf around 3:30p. Colonel R.F. Catterson of the 97th Indiana Infantry took command. Most of the Union casualties in the battle were from Confederate artillery.

The brave Militia members tried three more attacks. All failed, although Anderson's attack on the Union right came close to success late in the fight:

> After the action had progressed for some hours, Genl. Anderson took the detachment of his men that had been cut off [by the deep railroad cut], and went round to the enemy's right flank, when a most spirited and desperate fight ensued, lasting some hour and a half or more; but the enemy was too firmly established, and the general's force too small to dislodge him.[33]

During the battle, Catterson received reinforcements – an infantry regiment, and squadrons of Kilpatrick's Cavalry.

In Georgia in November, it starts to get dark around 5:00. As darkness descended over the battlefield, Philips retreated towards Griswoldville, where he was ordered back to Macon. By 2:00a on November 23, 1864, Philips and his men were back in Macon.

After the battle, the Union infantry examined the dead and wounded Militia soldiers. Most of them were old men, and boys under 15. The Union soldiers provided water and blankets to the wounded men, and left them on the field to be cared for by locals.

Casualty numbers during the Civil War are always hard to pin down. Union casualties were around 100, with 12-13 dead, and the rest wounded. Confederate casualties were 51 dead, and around 472 wounded.

---

[33] *The Siege of Savannah*, by Charles Colcock Jones (Joel Munsell, 1874)

Assessment of the Battle of Griswoldville

How should one assess the Battle of Griswoldville from the point of view of the South? Philips was inexperienced, possibly drunk at the time of the attack, and had clearly disobeyed orders[34] from his superior Gustavus Smith. After the War, Gustavus Smith commented on the failure of Philips to follow his orders:

> Early on the morning of the 22d the militia moved in compliance with Hardee's order; I remained in Macon a few hours for the purpose of procuring ammunition, supplies, and transportation, having ordered the senior brigadier-general present with the troops to halt before reaching Griswoldville and wait for further orders. He was instructed not to engage the enemy, but, if pressed, to fall back to the fortifications of East Macon; or, if necessary, toward the south in the direction already taken by Wheeler's cavalry. Contrary to my instructions the militia became engaged about one mile beyond Griswoldville, and were badly cut up. They lost 51 killed and 472 wounded, but they remained in close contact with the enemy until dark.[35]

Philips launched a frontal attack across an open field against an entrenched enemy on the heights at the end of that field, knowing that he was facing battle-hardened veterans of Sherman's army, while having inexperienced and poorly trained recruits in his own force. By that time in the War, after the experience of Fredericksburg, and Pickett's Charge at Gettysburg, the days of mass wave attacks against entrenched positions were pretty much over (hence the trench warfare at Petersburg).

Orders from Philips were garbled and poorly understood. Philips himself comments on this in his official report, using phrases such as "From some misconception of orders, when the general advance was being made, Genl. Anderson's brigade faced to the right and swept across the rail road ..." and "The order to Major Cook (from some cause of which I am not aware) to turn the enemy's left, was

---

[34] To not engage the enemy
[35] *Battles and Leaders of the Civil War Volume Four*, by Robert Underwood Johnson and Clarence Clough Buel (New York, Century Co., 1888)

never carried out..."[36] All of these factors would indicate that Philips was a very bad General. He makes my list of the five worst Confederate generals of the Civil War.

A contrarian view, though, cuts a little slack towards Philips. As foolishly conceived as the attack was, there were a few moments where victory would have been possible, especially when Cook's men and the State Line charged the Union left, and were driven back only after their own side mistakenly started firing at them. And later in the battle, the attack of General Anderson's forces on the Union right came close to success. If Cook and/or Anderson had been successful, the whole nature of the attack would have been different, and the Militia might have taken the day. General Philips commented on the importance of the flanking movements in his report:

> I can but believe if the flank movement had been carried out with all the forces assigned to that duty, that it would have resulted in dislodging and probably routing the enemy, notwithstanding he was, I am satisfied, fully equal if not superior to our forces. Whilst we have to regret the loss of many gallant officers and men, yet we cannot but hope that they died not in vain. [37]

And if the attack had been successful, no one would have complained that Philips disobeyed orders – he would have been complimented on his ability to adapt to changing conditions in the field. Sherman, for example, had been ordered by Grant to abandoned his assault on Savannah in December of 1864, and bring his army north to help Grant fight Lee. Sherman ignored the order, and took Savannah. No one criticizes Sherman for taking Savannah against orders from his superior.

So, ultimately, Philips was a poor general, and shouldn't have ordered the charge. But battles are games of inches, and his ragtag group of old men and young boys at least had a small chance of actually winning the day, an outcome that would have conceivably wreaked havoc on the supply lines of Sherman's Right Wing.

---

[36] *The Siege of Savannah*, by Charles Colcock Jones (Joel Munsell, 1874)
[37] *Ibid*

By that point of the War, members of the Georgia Militia were often derided by Southern newspapers and Confederate regulars for being poorly trained, poorly equipped, and in poor physical condition. On that day in Griswoldville, the Georgia Militia acquitted itself admirably, as they would at the Battle of Honey Hill a month later in South Carolina.

Sherman said later that the battle at Griswoldville was the only thing on the March to the Sea that was much like a fight:

> The affair at Griswoldville, where one brigade of infantry was engaged, and Kilpatrick's punishment of Wheeler, were the only things on the march like a fight. (William Tecumseh Sherman)[38]

---

[38] *Official Record*

Sherman's March to the Sea – End Game and Aftermath

The Georgia Militia troops that fought bravely at Griswoldville were reunited with their commander, Gustavus Smith and the First Brigade of Georgia Militia in a battle to defend Savannah. Their job was to prevent the Union from cutting off the railroad that ran from the west side of the Savannah River to Charleston. If this railroad could have been captured by the Union, Hardee would have been cut off, and have no way to receive supplies or escape (thanks, partly, to the Union capture of Fort Pulaski in 1862).

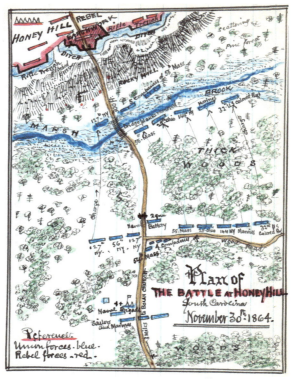

The Battle of Honey Hill[39]

---

[39] Library of Congress http://hdl.loc.gov/loc.ndlpcoop/gvhs01.vhs00181

The battle, known as the Battle of Honey Hill, took place near Grahamville, South Carolina on November 30, 1864. The Georgia Militia troops commanded a small rise, and several Federal attacks were not able to dislodge the Georgia Militia. The railroad route was protected, and Hardee was later able to escape into South Carolina.

Sherman had marched out of Atlanta on November 15, 1864. By December 12, Sherman's forces were arrayed against Savannah's defenses. The 275 mile March had taken less than a month to accomplish, with no supply line. But for the March to have been worth it, Savannah must fall.

Arrayed against Sherman's 60,000+ men, General William Hardee had a heavily entrenched 10,000 troops. Just as important to the Confederate defense of Savannah was the earthen-walled Fort McAllister, which guarded the Ogeechee River. If Sherman could take Fort McAllister, he could link up with the Union supply ships off the coast.[40]

Fort McAllister was heavily fortified, but had only 200 troops manning it. On December 13, 1864, troops under General William Hazen stormed the fort, and took it in a battle lasting all of 15 minutes. Almost simultaneously, Sherman linked up for the first time with the Union navy. For all intents and purposes, Savannah was Sherman's for the taking.

On December 15, 1864, Sherman ordered Howard and Slocum to prepare for an assault on Savannah. Sherman sent a surrender ultimatum to Hardee, which was politely refused.

On December 20, under orders from Beauregard, Hardee started evacuating his troops from Savannah using a pontoon bridge across the Savannah River. The bridge ran roughly on the same route as the modern Eugene Talmadge Memorial Bridge (Highway 17). By

---

[40] After the demonstration of what rifled cannon could do to a fort made out of brick in 1862 at Fort Pulaski, most forts built after that had earth walls, which easily absorbed cannon fire.

morning on December 21, Savannah was empty of Confederate resistance, and Sherman's troops started to enter the city.

c. 1864 drawing showing "Gen Sherman reviewing his army in Savannah before starting on his new campaign"[41]

Sherman contacted Grant with the happy news that Savannah had fallen – with hardly a shot fired:

> DEAR GENERAL: I take great satisfaction in reporting that we are in possession of Savannah and all its forts...Our troops entered at daylight yesterday, took about 800 prisoners, over 100 guns (some of the heaviest caliber), and a perfect string of forts from Savannah around to McAllister, also 12,000 bales of cotton, 190 cars, 13 locomotives, 3 steam-boats, and an immense supply of shells, shot, and all kinds of ammunition. There is a complete arsenal here, and much valuable machinery. The citizens mostly remain, and the city is very quiet.[42]

On Christmas Eve, 1864, Sherman sent a wire to President Abraham Lincoln:

---

[41] Library of Congress http://www.loc.gov/pictures/item/2004661239
[42] *Official Record*

I beg to present you, as a Christmas gift, the city of Savannah, with 150 heavy guns and plenty of ammunition, and about 25,000 bales of cotton.[43]

Savannah had fallen.

Results

All of Sherman's objectives were achieved through the March to the Sea. He destroyed the railroads in central Georgia, dealt a blow to the morale of the Confederacy from which it would never recover, he split the Confederate forces still left in Georgia, and he took Savannah a little over a month after leaving Atlanta. His Atlanta Campaign took four months to cover half the distance.

Sherman discusses his results in the Official Record:

> I was thereby left with a well-appointed army to sever the enemy's only remaining railroad communications eastward and westward, for over 100 miles-namely, the Georgia State Railroad, which is broken up from Fairburn Station to Madison and the Oconee, and the Central Railroad, from Gordon clear to Savannah with numerous breaks on the latter road from Gordon to Eatonton and from Millen to Augusta, and the Savannah Gulf Railroad. We have also consumed the corn and fodder in the region of country thirty miles on either side of a line from Atlanta to Savannah, as also the sweet potatoes, cattle, hogs, sheep and poultry, and have carried away more than 10,000 horses and mules, as well as a countless number of their slaves. **I estimate the damage done to the State of Georgia and its military resources at $100,000,000 [multiple billions in today's money]; at least, $20,000,000 of which has inured to our advantage, and the remainder is simple waste and destruction.** This may seem a hard species of warfare, but it brings the sad realities of war home to those who have been directly or indirectly instrumental in involving us in its attendant calamities. (emphasis added)[44]

---

[43] *Official Record*
[44] *Ibid*

Griswoldville Battlefield today

The battlefield is now a Georgia Historic Site, with a small monument and kiosk explaining the battle. Griswoldville itself is located several miles west of the the battlefield. There are several Georgia Historical Markers there, including one that discusses the pistol factory that was destroyed by Sherman's troops.

Griswoldville Battlefield

Location: "Griswoldville Battlefield is located east of Griswoldville in Twiggs County, Georgia, 10 miles east of Macon via U.S. 80 and Ga. Hwy. 57 towards Gordon on Baker Road."[45] From SR57, we turned north on Battlefield Drive, west (left) on Griswoldville Road, and right on Baker Road.

---

[45] http://www.gastateparks.org/core/item/page.aspx?s=153653.0.1.5

Appendix A – The Destruction of Griswoldville

Excerpts from the official record give a fuller description of what was destroyed at Griswoldville on November 20-21:

CENTRAL RAILROAD COMPANY,
Savannah, November 21, 1864.
Major - General McLAWS:
...I received the following from Augusta, from our operator at Gordon, written yesterday:

The lumber train was captured at Griswoldville and burned today. Negroes all safe. Destroyed the machine shops and foundry and Georgia Chemical Works. Road burned at Griswoldville.
Very respectfully, your obedient servant,
R. R. CUYLER,
President.[46]

November 21. - 1 water-tank, 13 railroad cars, 3 sets engine drivers, 12 car wheels, 20 tons wrought iron destroyed at Griswold, Ga.[47]

November 21. - 1 pistol factory, 1 soap factory, 1 candle factory, 1 foundry, in employ of rebel Government, 400 boxes soap, destroyed at Griswold, Ga. ; 12 wagons and carts, and 1 wagon load carpenter's tools, Government property, destroyed at Griswold, Ga. ; 1 shoe-blacking factory destroyed at Griswold, Ga. W. H. DAY, Captain and Provost-Marshal, Third Cavalry Division.[48]

We have destroyed a large amount of cotton, the Planters' Factory, a pistol factory and a mill at Griswold, the latter three by General Kilpatrick. Major General W. T. Sherman, Commanding Military Division of the Mississippi.

November 21, took position at Griswoldville; skirmish mildly all day, being in position, tearing up track, destroying a pistol and soap factory of much value to the enemy; E. H. MURRAY, Colonel Third Kentucky Cav. , Commanding 1st Brigadier , 3rd

---

[46] *Official Record*
[47] *Ibid*
[48] *Ibid*

Cav. Div. , Military Division of the Mississippi. [Captain L. G. ESTES, Assistant Adjutant-General.][49]

After night-fall we moved toward Griswoldville and encamped [November 20]. The next morning we moved to that point and commenced, with other portions of the command, the destruction of the railroad. Several miles of track were torn up, the ties burned, and the rails bent. The depot, several manufacturing establishments, and a large amount of machinery were also destroyed. During our stay some skirmishing (in which we were not engaged) occurred. R. H. KING, Lieutenant-Colonel, Commanding Third Kentucky Cavalry. Captain JAMES BEGGS, Actg. Asst. Adjt. General , First Brigadier , Third Cavalry Div.[50]

---

[49] *Ibid*
[50] *Ibid*

Appendix B - Descriptions of the Battle from the *Official Record*

We took our position to the right of the Sixth Iowa, the Ninety-seventh Indiana on our right. Here we rested and at 1 p. M. the skirmishers were attacked by the enemy's advance and driven. A strong line was soon seen forming on the west side of the field, and advanced. At this time my regiment had no works for defense, but hastily constructed a small, temporary line of works and awaited the approaching enemy, who was advancing in column by brigades. As soon as they came within range of our muskets a most terrific fire was poured into their ranks, doing fearful execution. Still they moved forward to a ravine which ran in front of the line, within forty-five yards of the works. Here they attempted to reform their line again, but so destructive was our fire that they were compelled to retire. At one time it seemed that they would overcome our thin line, as our ammunition [was] nearly exhausted and none nearer than two miles, but fortunately a sufficient amount was procured, and our boys kept up a continual fire for nearly three hours, when skirmishers were sent forward to capture any of the enemy left on the field. A few prisoners were brought in, besides a number of wounded. In our front were, by actual count, 51 of the enemy killed and wounded. (A. Willison, Major, commanding 103rd Illinois Volunteers[51])

I ordered General Woods to have General Walcutt's command rallied and take a defensive position near the open field mentioned above. The position selected was in the edge of the timber and along a slight rise in the ground, at the base of which a kind of marshy swamp formed a natural obstruction to the approach; the right and left of the position was pretty well secured by swamps, &c. Light breast-works, built of rails, were put up to cover our men, and a section of artillery of Captain Arndt's (First Michigan) battery was ordered there. These preparations were considered sufficient to meet any of General Wheeler's reconnaissances, which he might undertake after finding out that he was no longer pressed, but had to stand a more severe trial. In the afternoon the rebel commander brought forward four brigades of infantry and a battery of artillery,

---

[51] *Official Record*

supported by a strong cavalry force, to dislodge General Walcutt from his position. For several hours their attempts were repeated with the greatest impetuosity. Their artillery threw a terrific fire into the frail works of Walcutt, while their columns of infantry marched in heroic style to within fifty yards of our line. It was all in vain! Walcutt and his brave brigade proved that superior skill, coolness, and valor made up for the great disparity in numbers. When night came the enemy retired, leaving over 300 dead on the battle-field and a number of wounded, who were taken care of by our medical corps; also a number of prisoners were taken. Our loss was comparatively light. The brave General Walcutt was wounded by a piece of shell during the fight, and Colonel Catterson assumed the command of the brigade. (P. Jos. Osterhaus, Major-General, U. S. Volunteers[52])

I then, by direction of General Osterhaus, drew General Walcutt's brigade back to a strong position on the Duncan farm, and posted it in the edge of the woods, with open fields in front, the flanks resting near a swamp, impassable except at one or two points, and directed temporary works of rails and logs to be thrown up. About 2 o'clock the enemy attacked with infantry (militia), three lines deep, and numbering about 5,000, four pieces of artillery (12-pounder Napoleons), and two brigades of Wheeler's cavalry in reserve. The enemy moved across the open fields in three compact lines and gained a ravine within seventy-five yards of our works, from which they made three assaults, but met each time with a bloody repulse. The fight continued until sundown, when retired, leaving their dead and wounded on the field. Shortly after dark the brigade was withdrawn to the position near the church. About the middle of the engagement Brigadier General C. C. Walcutt was wounded severely in the lower part of leg; he retired from the field, and Colonel R. F. Catterson, Ninety-seventh Indiana Infantry, assumed command of the brigade. He showed marked ability in the manner in which he handled the troops. Shortly after the engagement opened the section of the battery was withdrawn on account of the severe fire from the enemy's lines, then within 100 yards of our position, and very destructive to the men and horses of the battery. About 4 o'clock I sent Major Baldwin, Twelfth Indiana Infantry (First Brigade), to report his regiment to Colonel Catterson, who put him on the right of his line to prevent the enemy from turning that flank. I also applied to Colonel Murray for some cavalry to cover the

---

[52] *Official Record*

flanks; he kindly sent a regiment on each flank, covering and watching the crossing of the swamp.

I cannot speak in too high terms of the coolness and gallantry of Brigadier General C. C. Walcutt and Colonel R. F. Catterson, Ninety-seventh Indiana Infantry. The skill with which they handled the troops and the results obtained show them to be men of marked ability.

The rebel loss, as near as could be ascertained without actual count, was 300 killed and from 700 to 1,200 wounded. Major-General Philips, Colonel Munn, Fifth Georgia, and Colonel George, are reported by the prisoners taken to have been killed, and Brigadier-General Anderson to have been wounded. Twenty-eight prisoners were captured and turned over to the provost-marshal of the army corps. Fifteen wounded were brought in and left at a house, not having transportation for them. Our loss was 13 killed, 79 wounded, and 2 missing. (Chas. R. Woods, Brigadier-General of Volunteers)[53]

Proceeding about one mile we met the enemy's cavalry, under Wheeler, and drove them beyond Griswold. The object of the reconnaissance having been accomplished the brigade was retired about one mile and took position at a point known as Duncan's farm. The enemy seeing this move followed up with three brigades of militia, numbering in all between 6,000 and 7,000 men. We had scarcely taken position in the edge of timber skirting the farm on the east when our pickets were fired upon. The brigade, thus posted behind a light barricade of rails hastily prepared after our pickets were driven in, lay anxiously awaiting his appearance. He was soon discovered emerging from the woods about 800 yards from our position, and rapidly running across an open field toward us in three lines of battle, either of which more than covered our brigade front. General Walcutt ordered Captain Arndt, of the First Michigan, Battery B, to open fire upon them, which he did with one section of his battery in position on the road near the center of our line, which was replied to sharply by four guns of the enemy in the open field, at a distance of about 800 yards, to the right and front, the first shot striking and damaging a caisson. On came the enemy, endeavoring to gain possession of a ravine running parallel to and about 100 yards to our front, but the fire was so terrible that ere

---

[53] *Ibid*

he reached it many of his number were stretched upon the plain. It was at this moment that General Walcutt received a severe wound and was compelled to leave the field. I immediately assumed command, and discovered the enemy moving to the right. I supposed he contemplated turning my right flank. As I had already disposed of every available man in the brigade, and my left so strongly pressed that not a man could be spared from it, I sent to the general commanding the division for two regiments. The Twelfth Indiana [was] immediately placed in position on the extreme right; also, a squadron of cavalry to watch the right and left flanks, but the day was already ours, as the enemy had been repulsed and driven from the field. I immediately sent forward a line of skirmishers, who succeeded in capturing about 42 prisoners and 150 small-arms. The battle commenced at 2.30 p.m. and lasted until sunset. During the engagement the enemy made three separate charges, and were as often repulsed with terrible slaughter.

I would gladly notice the many deeds of daring during the action, but to do so of every man who distinguished himself would be to mention each man by name in the brigade; but suffice it to say, the conduct of both officers and men was most superb.

The loss of brigade in killed was 14; in wounded, 42 -this number includes only those sent to hospital.

The loss of the enemy in killed and wounded could not have been less than 1,500, about 300 of whom were killed.

The total number of men engaged was 1,300. (Robert F. Catterson, Colonel, Ninety-seventh Indiana Infantry, commanding Brigade)[54]

---

[54] *Ibid*

Sources

- *Battles and Leaders of the Civil War Volume Four*, by Robert Underwood Johnson and Clarence Clough Buel (New York, Century Co., 1888)
- *Battles for Atlanta: Sherman Moves East*, by Ronald H. Bailey (Time-Life Books, 1985)
- *Fields of Glory: A History and Tour Guide of the Atlanta Campaign*, by Jim Miles (Rutledge Hill Press, 1989)
- *Griswoldville*, by William Harris Bragg (Mercer University Press, 2000)
- *Memoirs of General William T. Sherman*, 1875; reprinted by Da Capo Press, 1984
- *The Siege of Savannah*, by Charles Colcock Jones (Joel Munsell, 1874)
- *To the Sea: A History and Tour Guide of Sherman's March*, by Jim Miles (Rutledge Hill Press, 1989)
- *War of the Rebellion: Official Records of the Union and Confederate Armies*, U.S. Government Printing Office, 1891

Color photos by Robert Jones, unless otherwise noted.

Links

Library of Congress http://www.loc.gov/pictures/item/2003679761
Library of Congress http://www.loc.gov/pictures/item/94512493
Library of Congress http:hdl.loc.gov/loc.ndlpcoop/gvhs01.vhs00040
Library of Congress http://www.loc.gov/pictures/item/00652519/
Library of Congress http://www.loc.gov/pictures/item/det1994013530/PP/
Library of Congress http://www.loc.gov/pictures/item/cwp2003000446/PP/
Library of Congress http://www.loc.gov/pictures/item/brh2003002881/PP/
Library of Congress http://www.loc.gov/pictures/item/cwp2003004202/PP/
Library of Congress http://memory.loc.gov/cgi-bin/query/D?hlaw:1:./temp/~ammem_7dMg::
Library of Congress http://www.loc.gov/pictures/item/cwp2003004150/PP/
Library of Congress http://memory.loc.gov/cgi-bin/query/D?hlaw:2:./temp/~ammem_7dMg::
Library of Congress http://www.loc.gov/pictures/item/cwp2009000008/PP/
Library of Congress http://www.loc.gov/pictures/item/2002705763/
Library of Congress http://www.loc.gov/pictures/item/2004661205/
Library of Congress http://www.loc.gov/pictures/item/2004661820/
Library of Congress http://www.loc.gov/pictures/item/2004660966/
Library of Congress http://hdl.loc.gov/loc.ndlpcoop/gvhs01.vhs00181
Library of Congress http://www.loc.gov/pictures/item/2004661239
http://www.wikipedia.org

The Author on YouTube

There are several extracts of lectures by the author on Civil War topics available on YouTube, including:

Sherman's March: Strategy and Results
(http://www.youtube.com/watch?v=gAcqx0rpWXY)

Sherman's March: The Fall of Savannah
(http://www.youtube.com/watch?v=Iykjb7vA3wI)

Overview of the Great Locomotive Chase
(http://www.youtube.com/watch?v=CSJ03W8mlMc)

Author singing *"Hold the Fort"*
(http://www.youtube.com/watch?v=5LzWtVXAYAE)

All of these can be viewed in high definition (720p).

The author is available for lectures in Atlanta, North Georgia and Eastern Alabama. For details, see
http://www.rcjbooks.com/guest_speaker

Cover: Library of Congress
http://www.loc.gov/pictures/item/2004661205/

About the Author

Robert is President of the Kennesaw Historical Society, and Director of Programs and Education for the Kennesaw Museum Foundation. He is also on the advisory board of the Civil War Round Table of Cobb County. He has written several books on Civil War and railroad themes, including:

Battle of Allatoona Pass: The Forgotten Battle of Sherman's Atlanta Campaign, The
Battle of Chickamauga: A Brief History, The
Battle of Griswoldville: An Infantry Battle on Sherman's March to the Sea, The
Bleeding Kansas: The Real Start of the Civil War
Civil War Prison Camps: A Brief History
Confederate Invasion of New Mexico, The
Famous Songs of the Civil War
Fifteen Most Critical Moments of the Civil War, The
Pennsylvania Railroad: An Illustrated Timeline, The
Reading Railroad: An Illustrated Timeline, The
Retracing the Route of Sherman's Atlanta Campaign and March to the Sea
Top 20 Best – and Worst – Generals of the Civil War, The
Top 20 Civil War Spies and Irregulars, The
Top 20 Most Influential Leaders of the Civil War , The
Top 20 Railroad Songs of All Time, The
Top 25 Most Influential Women of the Civil War, The
W&A, the General, and the Andrews Raid: A Brief History, The

Robert has also written several books on "Old West" themes, including:

Death Valley Ghost Towns – As They Appear Today
Ghost Towns of Southern Arizona and New Mexico
Ghost Towns of the Mojave National Preserve
Ghost Towns of Western Nevada
Top 10 Gunslingers and Lawmen of the Old West, The

In 2005, Robert co-authored a business-oriented book entitled *Working Virtually: The Challenges of Virtual Teams*.

jone442@bellsouth.net
rcjbooks.com

CPSIA information can be obtained
at www.ICGtesting.com
Printed in the USA
LVHW072316200622
721742LV00001B/4